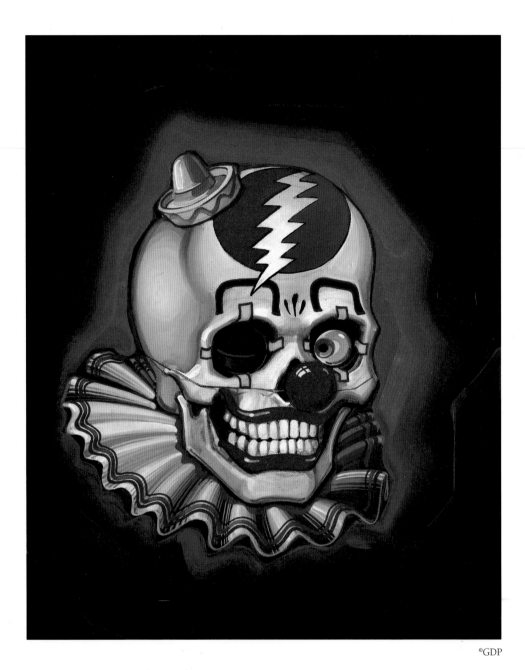

For Rick

DEAD DAYS

Herb Greene

"Grateful Dead Dancing Bears" copyright © 1990 Grateful
Dead Merchandising, Inc. "Grateful Dead Skeletons" copy-
right © 1992 Grateful Dead Merchandising, Inc./artwork by
Rick Griffen. "Without A Net" artwork copyright © 1990
Grateful Dead Merchandising, Inc./artwork by Rick Griffin.
"Steal Your Face™" is a registered trademark of Grateful
Dead Merchandising, Inc. "Grateful Dead" is a registered
service mark of Grateful Dead Productions, Inc.

Grateful Dead employee laminates and miscellaneous
line work are reproduced courtesy of Fine Line Design,
copyright © 1991.

Lyrics from "U.S. Blues," "Wharf Rat," "Box of Rain," "Eyes
of the World," "Dark Star," "Scarlet Begonias," "Candyman,"
"Friend of the Devil," and "Black Muddy River," reprinted
courtesy of Ice Nine Publishing Company, Inc., copyright
© Robert Hunter.

Lyrics from "I Need a Miracle," reprinted courtesy of
Ice Nine Publishing Company, Inc., copyright © by
John Barlow.

"One Afternoon Long Ago…" reprinted with permission
of Blair Jackson from the *Golden Road*.

"Grateful Dead Chronology" reprinted with permission
of Mike Dolgushkin from *Dead Base*, copyright © 1994

Album covers copyright © Grateful Dead
Productions, Inc.

Printed in Hong Kong through Global Interprint,
Petaluma, California

ISBN 0-9643831-1-X

Editing: Beth Haiken
Typesetting: Printed Page
Book and cover design: Ingalls + Associates
Designers: Kendra Lawrence and Carole Selig
Art Direction and Photography: Herb Greene

Editors note: The dates in this book are accurate to
the best of our knowledge at press time. Several album
release dates can be dated by month and year only.

Published by:
Global Interprint
2447 Petaluma Blvd. North
Petaluma, CA 94952

Distributed by Publishers Group West and Sourcebooks.

1967

"I need a woman 'bout twice my age
A lady of nobility, gentility, and rage,
A splendor in the dark, lightning on the draw,
We'll go right through the book
And break each and every law.
I got a feeling and it won't go away
Just one thing, then I'll be o.k.
I need a miracle everyday."

I Need a Miracle
John Barlow

One Afternoon Long Ago…

An Interview With Jerry Garcia, 1967

by Randy Groenke & Mike Cramer

There are surprisingly few Grateful Dead interviews available that took place before 1969. Of course, the rock press was just beginning in 1967, and the straight press all but ignored rock and roll. The most commonly circulated interview that deals with the Dead's Haight-Ashbury days is the Charles Reich-Jann Wenner *Rolling Stone* interview from late '71, several years down the line from the Haight's peak. So when Santa Cruz record collector/archivist Glenn Howard told me that he knew of a never-before-published tape interview with Garcia from early '67, my curiosity was piqued. Getting the tape proved to be a difficult task; however, it was ultimately dug out of storage several months later and many states away.

This interview was done at 710 Ashbury in February or March of 1967, just before the release of the Dead's first album. Randy Groenke, the principal interviewer, had been a banjo student of Garcia's in the early '60s when they both lived in the South Bay. He and his friend Mike Cramer simply called Jerry up and arranged to do the interview, friend to friend.

To set the scene: Garcia, Randy and Mike are talking in an upstairs room at 710. The band's equipment truck had been stolen the night before, so there is considerable commotion in the background about that. Weir drops by at one point, as does Mountain Girl, bearing a plate of Oreos. The conversation starts on the subject that first brought Randy and Jerry together – bluegrass.

–Blair Jackson

So you've left the bluegrass world completely, eh?
No, I'm re-entering it by way of the electric banjo. My banjo is in the process of being electrified.

Oh no! I never thought Garcia would go electric banjo! How does it sound, anyway? I'm really not familiar with it.
I haven't used it yet 'cause it's not finished. I played a friend of mine's who did it by means of a very simple operation involving a ceramic cartridge from a stereo taped underneath the bridge of the banjo. It sounds really good, better than a contact microphone or a magnetic pick-up microphone. It still sounds like a banjo, but an *electric* banjo. I don't know how I'm going to use it, but I'm going to use it. I also have another instrument, pedal steel guitar. I've been working on it about a month, and I should be using it with the band within about six weeks. [In fact he didn't play it publicly for nearly three years.] This is just an effort to broaden the scope a little, experiment a little. We're ready to experiment.

What do you like better, rock and roll or bluegrass?
I'm not saying what I like in terms of what I like to listen to. What I like to play is the music that we play. I don't want to call it rock and roll because it isn't exactly. It is, but it isn't. It's *our* music. We've developed it. We've developed our own sound, and it's our own music. That's what I'm into. I still listen to bluegrass. I don't listen to that much rock and roll. I listen to almost everything but rock and roll.

What do you think of the Airplane's stuff?
Well, their most recent album [Surrealistic Pillow] I'm kind of prejudiced in favor of because I'm on it. [Laughs]

You played flat-top on "My Best Friend" and "How Do You Feel?"
I played flat-top on "My Best Friend." Skip Spence played on the other one. He wrote that song. I played flat-top on "Plastic Fantastic Lover," and I played on "Coming Back to Me."

*That and "Today" I think are about the best tunes
on the album. What do you think?*
I'm kind of fond of the songs that Gracie sings. I
like the "White Rabbit" a lot. I like "Somebody to
Love." The arrangement on the album is more or
less my arrangement; I kind of rewrote it. I
always liked the song as she used to do it with
the Great Society, but the chord changes weren't
really very interesting.

*How do you think the sound of the Grateful Dead
fits in with what people are now calling the
"San Francisco Sound"?*
I'm not sure what they mean when they say the
"San Francisco Sound." I'd say we're a perfect
example of the "San Francisco Sound," since
we're from San Francisco. [Laughs] That term is
somebody's idea besides mine. There's similarity
in the sound of San Francisco groups because
they tend to do things kind of long, and they
tend to have a certain kind of sound because
you hear them in the same halls all the time.
But there really isn't that much similarity in the
musics of the bands. The Quicksilver Messenger
Service sounds a little more like us than, say, Big
Brother & the Holding Company. But neither of
them sounds very much like us. We don't sound
anything like Jefferson Airplane. It's a matter of

fine points. Superficially it might all sound similar, but actually, if you listen to the stuff, it's not
very similar.

*OK, let's take these San Francisco groups you
just mentioned and compare them with The Byrds
or The Animals and the English groups.*
It's different. It's a different sound. But each of
the San Francisco bands sounds as different from
each other as they do from everyone else. I think
the San Francisco music *scene* is healthier, and
there's more stuff going on in it than there is
anywhere else. The musicians are all young, and
we steal freely from each other because we all
play together and we're all friends. We all listen
to each other and we've all gotten good together.
We've all improved over the past year or so,
playing the same gigs the same weekends, getting together and jamming and so forth.

*What's your definition of a hippie? You hear so
much about it and people write it up…*
I'm not sure I have a definition. I'd say it's someone that's turned-on. And they can be turned-on
any way; like someone who's in forward motion.
They might have been called "progressive" at one
time. But it's motion and creative energy at its
best. It's just a better way for people who are in
a creative community to look at things.

*Do you like the term "psychedelic" to apply to
all of this?*
It could, but any of those kinds of terms could
apply, because I don't think the scene excludes
anything. I think it's more inclusive than exclu-
sive. Everyone has his own particular way of
going about things and getting things done. Our
way of doing things has to do with integrity and
how we feel about what we're doing. We've been
together for almost two years and we're only just
now making a record. And the reason we've
done it that way is that in the past we've had all
kinds of offers but we were never in a position to
be able to control what we were doing. But
because we held out, because we thought we
were worth something, now we can do anything
we want. We have control over our product. It's
not going to be chopped or changed. It's our stuff,

and because it's our stuff, we'll take full responsibility for it. Record companies don't want you to do that.

The point is we're just trying to make our music as well as we can and get it out, because we've created a demand for it to some extent. It's a matter of artistic pride with us, because it's the only thing we do – make music. So we devote a lot of time and energy and thought and actual work to it. We practice every day.

Do you think the Airplane have the same view, or do you think they're going more commercial?
I think they have the same view. If their stuff has a commercial thing it's because they've been victimized by the record company to a certain extent, in that they don't have a say… their producer decides what their sound will be like sometimes. Hopefully, that won't happen on their next album, though this last album was more a product of them than their producer [Dave Hassinger]. "But it was his idea to have a lot of echo and reverb, and they're really not too satisfied with it. But the Airplane is concerned about being musically good. They are really a talented organization. All the people in the Jefferson Airplane are professionals and good musicians, and they work well and have good ideas.

These kids who come down to Fillmore Auditorium – are they phonies or really in with the music?
Who knows? The point is that they're really people. Anything else that they are doesn't alter the fact they are really people. They're human beings. Like I was saying, I don't want to exclude anybody, or include anybody. Whether or not they're all musicians or music critics, I don't know. It doesn't matter to me because on the level of the musical part of it, there are musicians there who will recognize when something musically groovy happens. If they don't, *I* will. But for some reason with the music we're playing, when something groovy does happen, everyone knows about it. Nobody has to tell anybody, because it's obvious music. It's loud and there's excitement about it. But it's like reciprocal excitement. We pick it up from the audience, we feed it back to

them; it works back and forth. For any kind of music you play, it's always groovy to play for an audience that's responsive, and I find the audiences at the Fillmore Auditorium and the Avalon Ballroom to be pretty responsive. When something groovy gets going we can always depend on a little support. If that wasn't happening, the music wouldn't be as much fun to play.

If you were to go to New York right now, what do you think your reception would be like?
I don't know. We're going to New York pretty soon, so we'll find out. What we've heard from the people we know from New York who've been here is that we'd really kill 'em in New York. Whether or not that's so is something I don't know, because I don't know about New York and what it's like to play there.

Well, I guess it's a fact that this San Francisco music scene isn't anywhere else. Why is that? Why did it happen in San Francisco?
I don't know. Here's the thing: there really aren't that many musicians in San Francisco, but there is a fantastically good *scene* going on in San Francisco. San Francisco is a good place to live, and then, incidentally, a good place to play. But *first* it's a good place to live, and having that

Mushroom

place – where you can do what you want and feel the way you want – has something to do with your outlook on things.

The San Francisco music scene is unique in some aspects, socially. For example, there isn't any competition going on; the bands don't compete with each other. The bands do things to help each other. The managers don't do things the old cigar-chewing-manager way. When our managers [Danny Rifkin and Rock Scully] go someplace, they go just the way they are around the house. They have long hair, wear outlandish clothes and beads, and they talk like people on Haight Street do. Because that's the way they are. That's the way we *all* are, and we're not sacrificing any part of ourselves to do business. When we go into the business parts of things – when we talk to lawyers, the vice presidents of Warner Brothers – we talk to them the way we talk to our friends. We're being out front. We're trying to change the whole atmosphere of music, the business part as well as just the way it is, just by dealing with it on a more humanistic level because it's a valuable commodity – it's an art.

What did you think of that article in Newsweek, "Dropouts with a Mission"?
It surprised me that it was in Newsweek, but it didn't surprise me too much because they'd taken the pictures here and everything. If we hadn't known in advance that the article was going to be favorable, we wouldn't have consented to appear in pictures. But because it was favorable they got a good reception.

How about that title, "Dropouts with a Mission"?
I *am* a dropout. When I was teaching music, I was doing it because it was a way to exist without having to do a work thing – put on a collar and go do eight hours a day and all that stuff. I'm not interested in doing that. What I was interested in doing was making music, and I've been willing to put down everything else for that at one time or another. So in that case, socially I'm a dropout. But the result has been that because I was willing to take a chance and say "I want to play music and I don't care

Gary Snyder

what anybody else thinks about it," it put me in a position of where I'm starting to be successful at it, which I never *dreamed* I'd be. I was willing to work at it like I might have worked at a job, but I worked it out of love, and not because I had to eat or make car payments or any of that stuff.

If you'd had enough money to exist, would you have not taught and spent all your time with your music?
I might have. The teaching was valuable, though, because it made me think about what I was doing –

It was valuable to me!
– and it might have been valuable to a few others like you or any of my students. But it's not really my thing to be a teacher. My thing is to play.

What really made you quit pounding on the banjo and start playing guitar?
It was a gradual changeover. The main thing is, when I was playing the banjo there was nobody to play with and no place to play, no way for anyone to *hear* me. There wasn't enough popular interest in bluegrass music for it to ever be worthwhile in this area. That's what happens when you take up something that's pretty esoteric. You have to sort of accept that. I didn't want to do it.

I got into rock and roll music through the jug band. When I *first* started playing, I played rock and roll. My first guitar was electric, and I played Chuck Berry, stuff like that.

Allen Ginsberg

Michael McClure

I remember when you were The Warlocks and at Magoo's [a South Bay pizza parlor] you were doing stuff like "The Last Time" –
Right, popular stuff.

Did you have your sights on what you're doing now?
We didn't know what we were doing! We were just screwing around. We were just trying something.

Did music of The Beatles and Rolling Stones help you get into this?
For sure. Because The Beatles' music was interesting music. The Rolling Stones' music was not that much of a surprise, because I'd listened to a lot of rhythm & blues, and early Rolling Stones was similar to that music, although not as well done. But The Beatles were doing something new and they had great musical ideas and a great thing going. Plus, seeing the movie, *Hard Day's Night,* was a turn-on. It was very "up," and I've always preferred things that are a little on the "up" side.

If it comes along that you become successful and fairly wealthy –
– then we'll see if there's a better way to become successful and wealthy! A way that's more rewarding to us. A way to spend our money so that it brings about more enjoyment for more people, or more *something* for people. More food certainly. A lot of what we make now is just money to live on for us and our friends and anybody around who doesn't have anything. I don't need

anything. I don't really want anything. I've got instruments, I know I can eat, so there's nothing to worry about.

How is the war in Vietnam hitting you?
Well, not directly at all so far, except that it's getting hard to buy things like cymbals and guitar strings because they're making bullets out of them.

There's something going on in the world that nobody knows about. It's like a big mystery. But it's not *really* a mystery. The war is an effort on the part of the establishment to keep the economic situation in the United States comparatively stable.

If you had not already been in the service –
– would I go? I would not go. I am totally against war. I could never kill anybody. Killing might be the only "sin" that there is. It's anti-life. I don't see how *anybody* could do it. I don't feel like any kind of subversive force. I feel like an American, and I'm really ashamed of it lately.

Do you think your music is talking about those kinds of things?
We're trying to make music in such a way that it doesn't have a message for anybody. We don't have anything to tell anybody We don't want to change anybody. We want people to have the chance to feel a little better. That's the absolute most we want to do with our music. The music that we make is an act of love, an act of joy. We really like it a lot. If it says something, it says it

in its own terms at the moment we're playing it, and it doesn't have anything to do with…we're not telling people to go get stoned, or drop out. We're just playing, and they can take it any way they want.

In short phrases, name some "in" things and some "out" things, some things you like and don't like.
I can only tell you about things I like. There isn't that much that I don't like. I don't have any complaints.

What do you think of Buffalo Springfield?
I like them a lot. Have you heard Moby Grape? They're really good.

What do you think of The Monkees?
What am I *supposed* to think of them? [Laughs] I mean, what do you want me to say?

Well, I mean, why should they get to be Number One?
I don't know. Maybe because their records are really pretty good. They *should* be good, because they have the best L.A. studio musicians and the best arrangers…

You've heard your own [first] album by now. What do you think?
Well, I think our album is honest. It sounds just like us. It even has mistakes on it. But it also has a certain amount of excitement on it. It sounds like we felt good when we were making it. We made it in a short period – four days – and it's the material we've been doing onstage for quite a long time. It sounds like one of our good sets.

What do you think is going to happen to the San Francisco Scene?
I don't know. I'm not even sure why there's so much commotion, let alone what's going to happen to it.

All things come to an end, and things go "out" – like the English sound is sort of going out. What will you do if this goes out – switch back to bluegrass?
Who knows? I'll know that when I get there. It doesn't bother me now because the thing I'm most interested in is the thing that's going on around me now, not what might happen tomorrow or yesterday.

In that respect, you don't seem very concerned about the stuff [the band's equipment truck] that was taken.
Well, it's pointless to worry about it. I could work myself into a frenzy about it, but somebody stole it; it's gone. I hope they can have a good time with it. [Laughs] I hope we can get it back without having to put somebody in jail. It's not that big a thing, because we can afford to get more. And maybe that's some sort of spiritual dues that we paid for being successful; that means that now somebody can steal our equipment and not feel too guilty about it because we're making more money than they are.

As far as creativity goes, it seems like outside of music there really hasn't been that much going on.
There never is. But there is a small, heavily concentrated area of a lot of activity. There is a lot of creativity, but it's not always on levels you can observe because there are different trends happening in what we used to call "the arts." For example, six or seven years ago, if you were a painter in San Francisco, you never sold anything, because nobody in San Francisco buys paintings and there's no place to sell them. But a guy with a light show can make money. The guys who run the light shows are the guys who were painters a few years ago, and they're finding out something new about color, and the eye, and about spontaneity. Those are all aspects the plastic arts have never had before.

Poster design and printing, all those things, are skills. These posters here are a product of a lot of people's working at something, and they're getting a return for it. The people who run the dance halls are doing a thing. The people who are being managers are doing something. There's a lot going on. People are opening stores. Not everybody is an artist or a creative person, but not everyone has to be a bookkeeper or a businessman to make it. They can get into something that turns them on a little. With our scene here, we've managed to employ just about everyone we know in some capacity, because everybody has something they can do.

How do the Hell's Angels strike you?
I like 'em. They're honest and they're out front and they don't lie to you. They're good people. They're *brutal*, but their brutality is really only honesty. You have to know a few of them. They're kind of like the cops in a way. They have very heavy standards of what they do and what's right.

But by what you were saying before, you're not into that.
That's their scene, not my scene. They're also capable of not being brutal. They can be depended on in a funny way. When there was the Be-In up here [Jan. 14,1967] I'd never seen so many

people in my life. It was really fantastic. I almost didn't believe it. It was a totally underground movement. It was all the people into dope of any sort, and like 20,000 people came out in the park and everyone had a good time. There was no violence, no hassling. But one of the things that happened was that somebody came along and cut the lines of the p.a. and the electricity. Some guys got together to repair it, and then the Hell's Angels guarded the wire. They took care of lost kids, they baby sat! You can hit on 'em to do that kind of thing. Like we're hiring a couple to guard our warehouse, now that the equipment's been stolen.

I know that they're making a big change, that they're different than they used to be. They're hanging out in the scene and getting out of their brutal bags and just taking it easy a little.

Do you think they see what you guys are doing and then–
Well, they know that we're all doing the same thing. What we're saying is, "We don't want the world the way you've got it" – the establishment. We don't want to be successful or super-rich or businessmen. We don't want to do any of that shit. We want to have a nice quiet life and a few good times.

[Bob Weir comes in the room and announces that the Dead's equipment van has been found. There's much rejoicing.]

Here's another similar scene. We once played a ski shop, a very plush ski shop for this super-rich ski crowd. It was jet setters and what have you. Joan Baez was there. And the guy who owned the ski shop hired two Hell's Angels to guard the door to make sure nobody got in without an invitation. And they did it *fine*. And then the guy took us all out to dinner – us and the Hell's Angels. So we walked into this restaurant and lots of tourists split in horror, and this juiced San Francisco attorney came over and slapped us on the back and said [he slurs the words] "Glad you folks are here," and he bought us all wine. [Laughs]

Would you like to do a movie?
Well, as a matter of fact, when we were in L.A. making our record, we got a movie offer from ABC-Paramount. We got an offer to be in a James Coburn movie in which he plays the psychiatrist for the President, who runs off from his job for a series of misadventures, one of which is to spend a certain amount of time with us, with a rock and roll band that is traveling around in a nomadic fashion. We're written into the script, with speaking parts and everything. We've agreed to do it, provided we have control over the section we're in. So we might not do it because they might not give us control. We don't want to be in a movie unless it's good, and it won't be good unless we do it ourselves. [The film is *The President's Analyst*. Ultimately, the Dead were not in it.]

What do you get out of smoking dope?
Do you play better under it?
No, but I might feel better. I feel like if you want to have something that makes you feel a little better and maybe gives you a slightly different outlook than your normal one, it's nobody's business but yours. Grass is so much like an everyday thing. You don't get wasted on it.

How about LSD and the whole "Captain Trips" thing?
That's a whole 'nother matter. We've played on acid and that does do things to your time sense, and it does other things. It produces an unimaginably wider scope of ideas. More consciousness means you have more of an understanding of what you're doing, and that means you can do it better because you're doing it with that much more of your mind.

But you don't go down to the Fillmore or Avalon on acid…
Not anymore. We used to. I wouldn't do it anymore because we're in a different position than we were a year ago. At this point, the experimentation we're doing now isn't a matter of drug experimentation; we're experimenting with *music*.

Reprinted with permission of *The Golden Road*.

Front Street. Novermber 4, 1991

"Sometimes the **light's** all shining on me,
other times I can barely see."

Truckin, Robert Hunter

"New Year's Day Wail," Panhandle, San Francisco, CA 1/1/67

1

⚡ Oakland, CA 1/1/91

⚡ NYC, NY 1/2/70

2

3

4

5

6

First Madison Square Garden show, NYC, NY 1/7/79

7

January

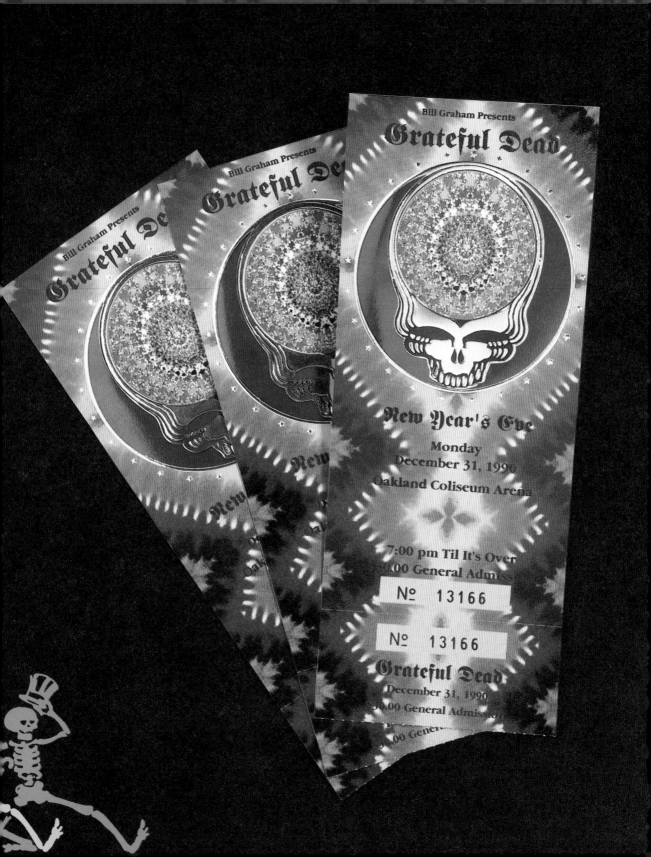

Grateful Dead 1966

"When the last bolt of sunshine hits the mountain
And the stars start to splatter in the sky
When the moon splits the southwest horizon
With the scream of an eagle on the fly"

Black Muddy River
Robert Hunter

8

9

10  Uniondale,
NY 1/10/79

11 Chico, CA
1/11/68

12

13

14 "Great Human Be-In,"
Golden Gate Park,
San Francisco, CA
1/14/67

January

15

16

First Carousel
Ballroom (later
Fillmore West) show,
San Francisco, CA
1/17/68

 Corvallis, OR
1/17/70

17

18

19

 Eureka, CA
1/20/68

20

21

January

"Trips Festival,"
Longshoremens Hall,
San Francisco, CA
1/22/66 – 1/23/66

22

 Honolulu, HI
1/23/70

23

24

25

26

27 Wolfgang Mozart 1/27/1756

28

January

Dylan/Dead 1987

1

 St. Louis, MO
2/2/70

2

 Portland, OR
2/3/68

3

4

5

Bob Marley 2/6/1945

6

Last show at
Henry J. Kaiser
Convention Center,
Oakland, CA 2/7/89

7

Phil 1969

February

Grateful Dead 1979

February

Neal Cassady 1966

February

15   *⚡* Philadelphia, PA 2/15/69

⚡ Madison, WI 2/15/73

16

17   Oakland Coliseum Arena "Rock for Life Benefit," Oakland, CA. Keith and Donna's last appearance with the band. 2/17/79

18   Capitol Theater, Port Chester, NY. Night of ESP experiment. Mickey leaves the band. 2/18/71

⚡ Port Chester, NY 2/18/71

19

20

Vince Welnick 2/21/1951   **21**

Vallejo, CA
2/22/69

22

  Champaign -
Urbana, IL
2/22/73

23

  Lake Tahoe,
CA 2/24/68

24

  San Francisco,
CA 2/24/74

25

 Lincoln, NB
2/26/73

26

 San Francisco,
CA 2/27/69

27

San Francisco,
CA 2/28/69

28

February

1966/1990

J. Garcia 1987

1 San Francisco, CA 3/1/69

2 San Francisco, CA 3/2/69

3 Free Show, Haight Street, San Francisco, CA 3/3/68

4

5

6

7

8

9

THE GRATEFUL DEAD
3/10/67

10

11

Bammies,
Civic Auditorium,
San Francisco, CA
3/12/88

12

13

14

March

Phil 1987

15 — San Francisco, CA 3/15/69 — Phil Lesh 3/15/1940

16 — San Francisco, CA 3/16/68 — Uniondale, NY 3/16/73

17 — San Francisco, CA 3/17/68 — Buffalo, NY 3/17/70

18

19 — Tom "TC" Constanten 3/19/1944

20

21 — Utica, NY 3/21/73

March

22

Cow Palace, Daly City, CA. First "Wall of Sound" gig. 3/23/74

23

"Snack" benefit, Kezar Stadium, San Francisco, CA 3/23/75

 NYC, NY 3/23/72

24

 Dania, FL 3/24/70

 Philadelphia, PA 3/24/73

25

 Location unknown 3/26/68

26

 Merced, CA 3/27/69

27

Essen, Germany, with The Who 3/28/81

28

 Springfield, MA 3/28/73

Rhythym Devils 1987

29 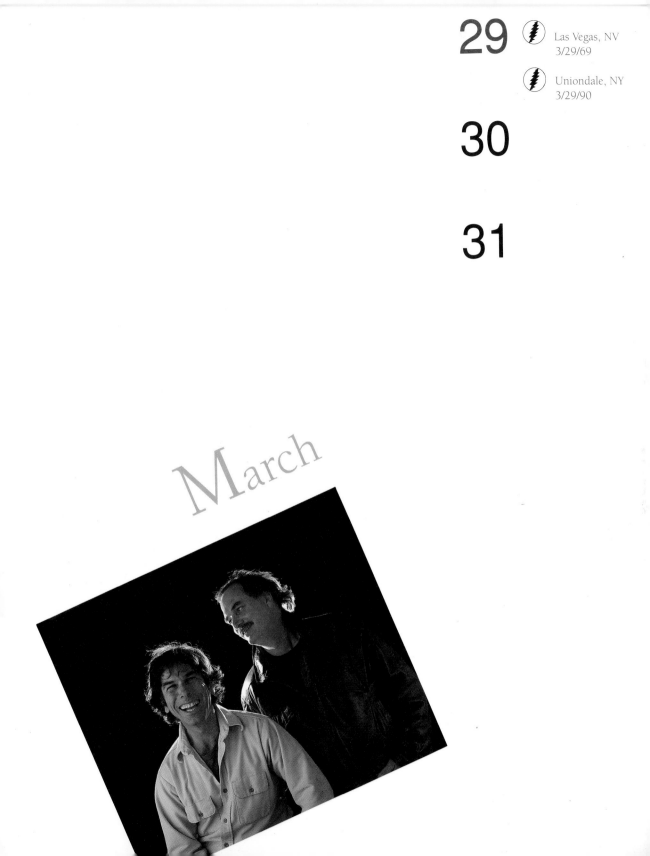 Las Vegas, NV
3/29/69

Uniondale, NY
3/29/90

30

31

March

Bob 1979

1

2

3

4 San Francisco,
CA 4/4/69

5 "Saturday Night Live."
Bobby wears bunny
ears. 4/5/80

San Francisco,
CA 4/5/69

6

7 Wembley Arena,
London. "Europe '72"
tour starts. 4/7/72

April

Boston, MA
4/8/71

 Wembley,
England 4/8/72

8

9

10

 San Francisco,
CA 4/11/70

11

12

 Boulder, CO
4/13/69

13

Lewisburg, PA
4/14/71

Copenhagen,
Denmark
4/14/72

14

April

Mickey 1967

Phil 1966

GRATEFUL DEAD

15

16

17

St. Louis, MO
4/17/69

Copenhagen,
Denmark
4/17/72

18

19

20

21

Boston, MA
4/21/69

April

Spartan Stadium, San Jose, CA. Brent's first show with the band. 4/22/79

22

 Boston, MA
4/22/69

23

 Boston, MA
4/23/69

 Denver, CO
4/24/70

24

 Dusseldorf, West Germany
4/24/72

 Denver, CO
4/25/70

25

 NYC, NY
4/26/71

26

 Minneapolis, MN 4/27/69

27

Go To Heaven
4/28/80

28

 NYC, NY
4/28/71

Grateful Dead 1987

Duke Ellington 4/29/1899

29

Last Fillmore East
performance, NYC,
NY 4/29/71

 Hamburg,
West Germany
4/29/72

30

The Warlocks 1965

"Walk out of any doorway
feel your way, feel your way
like the day before
Maybe you'll find direction
around some corner
where it is waiting to meet you—"

Box of Rain
Robert Hunter

May

May

1

2

3 Columbia University
during student strike,
NYC, NY 5/3/68

 San Francisco,
CA 5/3/69

4  Paris, France
5/4/72

5 Central Park, NYC,
NY 5/5/68

6 Outdoors at M.I.T.,
Cambridge, MA,
during student strike
in protest of Kent
State killings 5/6/70

Polo Field, Golden
Gate Park, San
Francisco, CA 5/7/69

Johannes Brahms 5/7/1833
Billy Kreutzman 5/7/1946

7 Last performance at
Frost Amphitheater,
Stanford University,
Palo Alto, CA 5/7/89

 San Francisco,
CA 5/7/69

 Manchester,
England
5/7/72

WORKINGMAN'S DEAD
5/70

8

First show at Laguna
Seca Raceway,
Monterey, CA 5/9/87

9

Pasadena, CA
5/10/69

10

Rotterdam,
The Netherlands
5/11/72

11

12

13

Missoula, MT
5/14/74

14

May

Jerry 1970

"Once in a while
you get shown the light
in the strangest of places
if you look at it right."

Scarlet Begonias
Robert Hunter

15 ⚡ NYC, NY
5/15/70

16

17

18 "Northern California
Folk-Rock Festival,"
Santa Clara, CA
5/18/68

⚡ Munich,
West Germany
5/18/72

19 First show at Avalon
Ballroom,
San Francisco, CA
5/19/66

20

21

May

22

 London,
England
5/23/72

23

"Hollywood
Festivals," Newcastle-
Under-Lyme,
England. First
appearance overseas.
5/24/70

24

 Newcastle-
Under-Lyme,
England
5/24/70

 London,
England
5/25/72

25

Strand Lyceum,
London, England.
"Europe '72" tour
ends. 5/26/72

26

27

Vietnam Veterans'
benefit, Moscone
Center, San Francisco,
CA 5/28/82

28

 May

29 HISTORIC DEAD
5/71

30 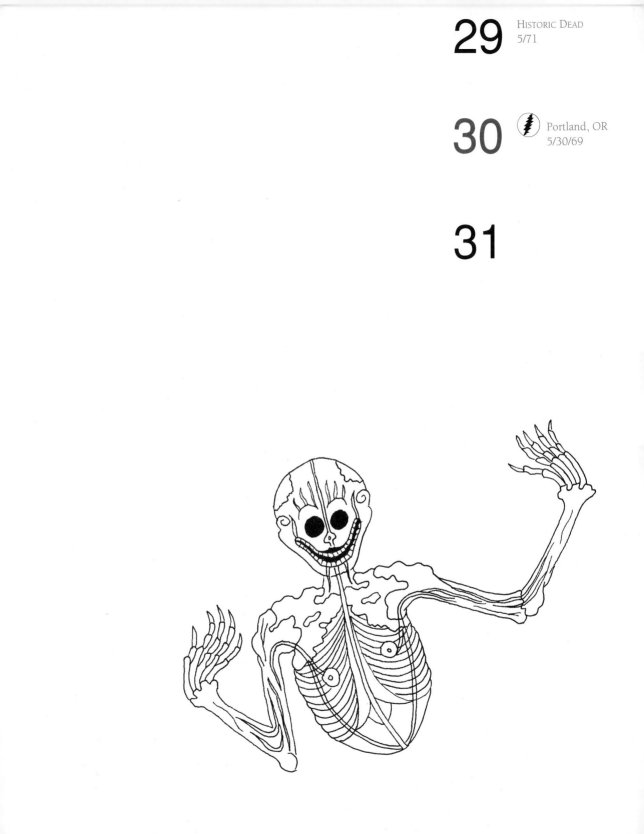 Portland, OR
5/30/69

31

GRATEFUL DEAD

1989

SUMMER

ACCESS ALL AREAS

Laminate art by Tim Harris
Tie-dye by Not Fade Away Graphics

Tompkins Square
Park, NYC, NY. First
New York appearance.
6/1/67

1

Billy 1967

2

Paramount Theater,
Portland, OR. The
Dead resume touring.
6/3/76

3

4

5

6

"Fifteenth
Anniversary
Celebration," Folsom
Field, Boulder, CO
6/7/80 – 6/8/80

7

 San Francisco,
CA 6/7/68

June

Vince Welnick 1991

June

8

9   First performance at
Cal. Expo.
Amphitheater,
Sacramento, CA
6/9/84

10    Washington,
DC 6/10/73

11

12

13

First Fillmore East
performance, NYC,
NY 6/14/68

14   20th Anniversary
Show, Greek Theater,
Berkeley, CA. "Sgt.
Pepper's" is played
before show at full
volume, rendering
much of P.A. system
useless. 6/14/85

 Monterey, CA
6/14/69

GD · XXV · AD

ANNO EQUUS

15

16

17 Hollywood Bowl,
Hollywood, CA.
Pigpen's last
performance. 6/17/72

18 Phil's first gig.
Frenchy's, Hayward,
CA. 6/18/65

Monterey Pop
Festival, Monterey, CA
6/18/67

19 Anchorage, AK
6/19/80 – 6/21.80

20 AOXOMOXOA
6/20/69

21 Chateau D'Herouville,
Herouville, France.
First performance on
European mainland.
6/21/80

Mickey and Taro 1987

June

Central Park, NYC,
NY 6/22/69

22

 NYC, NY
6/22/69

 Miami, FL
6/23/74

23

 Port Chester,
NY 6/24/70

24

25

STEAL YOUR FACE
6/26/76

26

MARS HOTEL
6/27/74

27

 Santa Rosa, CA
6/27/69

First appearance at
Oakland Auditorium
(later Henry J. Kaiser
Convention Center),
Oakland, CA 6/28/67

28

June

GRATEFUL DEAD FROM THE MARS HOTEL

Jerry 1967

Captain Trips 1966

"Wave that flag
Wave it wide and high
Summertime done come and gone
My, oh, my
Summertime done come and gone
My, oh, my"

U.S. Blues
Robert Hunter

1

2 Last appearance at
Fillmore West,
San Francisco, CA
7/2/71

3

4 First "Dylan and The
Dead" gig. Foxboro,
MA 7/4/87

5

6 IN THE DARK
7/6/87

7 First show at Red
Rocks Amphitheater,
Morrison, CO 7/7/78

July

8

9

10

11

 Washington,
DC 7/12/90
12

BEAR'S CHOICE 7/13/73
 Berkeley, CA
7/13/84
13

14

Bob Weir 1986

July

15

16

First show in
Ventura, CA 7/17/82

17

ANTHEM OF THE SUN
7/18/68

 Jersey City, NJ
7/18/72

18

19 Keith Godchaux
7/19/1948

20

21

J uly

Mickey 1987

22

23

24

⚡ Chicago, IL
7/25/74

25

26

Watkins Glen, NY
7/27/73 – 7/28/73

27

TERRAPIN STATION
7/27/77

28

July

29 Vancouver, BC. First
show outside of U.S.
7/29/66

30

31 Last show at Laguna
Seca Raceway,
Monterey, CA
7/31/88

New Haven,
CT 7/31/71

Bob,

Brent,

Bill,

and Phil 1987

"Wake up to find out
that you are the eyes of the world"

Eyes of the World
Robert Hunter

Jersey City, NJ
8/1/73

1   Jerry Garcia 8/1/1942

2

3

4

5

6

7

J. Garcia 1966

August

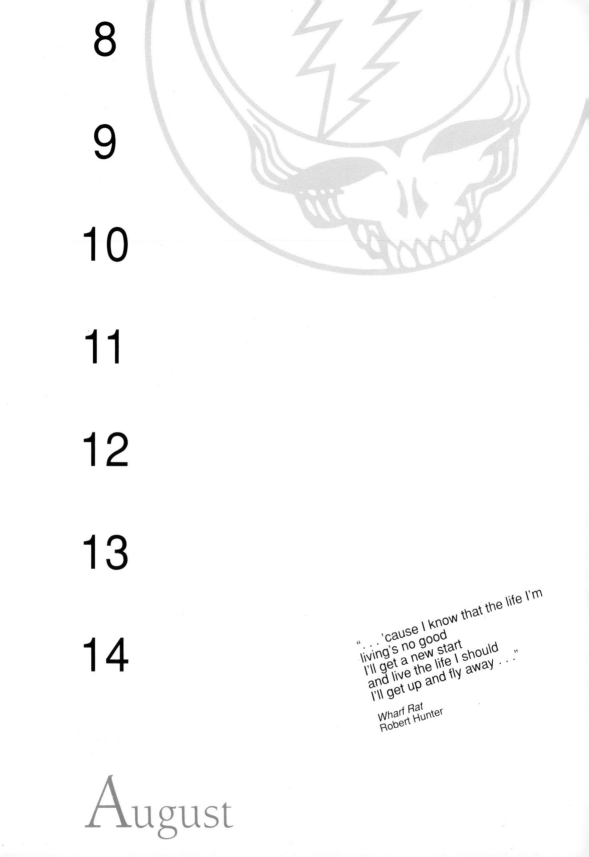

8

9

10

11

12

13

14

" . . . 'cause I know that the life I'm
living's no good
I'll get a new start
and live the life I should
I'll get up and fly away . . . "

Wharf Rat
Robert Hunter

August

Pig 1969

Mickey and Billy 1969

August

15

16   Woodstock, NY
         8/16/69

17

18

19   Last show at Greek
         Theater, Berkeley, CA
         8/19/89

20    San Francisco,
         CA 8/20/68

21   San Francisco,
         CA 8/21/68

         Berkeley, CA
         8/21/72

Donna Godchaux 8/22/1947

 San Francisco,
CA 8/22/68

22

First show at Alpine
Valley Music Theater,
East Troy, WI 8/23/80

23

 Los Angeles,
CA 8/23/68

 Los Angeles,
CA 8/24/68

24

25

26

Springfield Creamery
benefit, Veneta, OR
8/27/72

27

 Veneta, OR
8/27/72

Springfield Creamery
presents "Second
Decadenal Field Trip,"
Veneta, OR 8/28/82

28

 San Francisco,
CA 8/28/68

August

29 San Francisco,
CA 8/29/69

30 San Francisco,
CA 8/30/69

31

Jerry 1969

GRATEFUL DEAD

Fall
1989
Winter

ACCESS ALL AREAS

Laminate art by Tim Harris
Tie-dye by Joyce Kuchar

BLUES FOR ALLAH
9/1/75

1

DEAD SET
9/1/81

 Prairieville, LA
9/1/69

2

"Sky River Festival,"
Sultan, WA 9/2/68

 Sultan, WA
9/2/68

3

Raceway Park,
Englishtown, NJ
9/3/77

 Rio Nido, CA
9/4/67

4

US Festival, Devore,
CA 9/5/82

5

6

7

Grateful Dead 1966

September

Mountain Girl and Garcia

September

Ron "Pigpen" McKernan
9/8/1945

8

9 London, England.
"Europe '74" tour
starts. 9/9/74

10  Hollywood,
CA 9/10/72

 London,
England
9/10/74

Mickey Hart 9/11/1943 **11**  Williamsburg,
VA 9/11/73

12

13

14 Cairo, Egypt
9/14/78 – 9/16/78

15

16  Boston, MA
9/16/72

17 NYC, NY
9/17/70

18

19 NYC, NY
9/19/70

20 NYC, NY
9/20/90

21 Paris, France.
"Europe '74" tour
ends. 9/21/74

 Philadelphia,
PA 9/21/72

September

22

23

Rainforest benefit,
Madison Square
Garden, NYC, NY
9/24/88

24

 Waterbury, CT
9/24/72

The Dead start a
fifteen night run at
the Warfield Theater,
San Francisco, CA.
They revive acoustic
sets. 9/25/80

25

26

 Jersey City, NJ
9/27/72

27

Lindley Meadows in
Golden Gate Park,
San Francisco, CA
9/28/75

28

September

29 Straight Theater, San Francisco, CA. Mickey joins the band. 9/29/67

30 Edinburgh, Scotland. "Europe '81" tour starts. 9/30/81

Grateful Dead 1967

Mickey 1985

First show at Greek Theater, Berkeley, CA 10/1/67

1

First gig at Shoreline Amphitheater, Mountain View, CA. The 20th anniversary of 710 Ashbury bust. They play "Truckin." 10/2/87

2

3

Winterland, the night Janis Joplin dies 10/4/70

4

5

"Lunatic Protest Demonstration," Panhandle, San Francisco, CA. LSD becomes illegal in California. 10/6/66

6

First performance at Winterland, San Francisco, CA 10/7/66

7

October

VINTAGE DEAD
10/70

8

"Dead Roadies'
Benefit," Winterland,
San Francisco, CA
10/9/72

9

First show at Frost
Amphitheater,
Stanford University,
Palo Alto, CA
10/9/82

 San Francisco,
CA 10/9/68

10

 Hampton, VA
10/9/89

Oakland Stadium
with The Who,
Oakland, CA
10/9/72 – 10/10/72

11

 San Francisco,
CA 10/10/68

 Paterson, NJ
10/11/70

12

 San Francisco,
CA 10/13/68

13

14

October

MAREK LIEBERBERG & OSSY HOPPE PRESENT

GRATEFUL DEAD

EUROPE 1990

Montag, 22. Oktober 1990 · 20.00 Uhr

FRANKFURT · FESTHALLE

Vorverkauf: DM 40,–
zuzügl. Vorverkaufsgebühr, inkl. 7 % MwSt.,
zuzüglich DM 1,– für die Leistungen des FVV.

Abendkasse: DM 46,–
inkl. 7 % MwSt.

KEIN SITZPLATZANSPRUCH!

FVV-Ticket für die Hin- und Rückfahrt. Gültig auf allen FVV-Linien für 1 Fahrt
in der 2. Klasse zur Festhalle Frankfurt und zurück. Hinfahrt frühestens 3 Stunden
vor Veranstaltungsbeginn, Rückfahrt bis Betriebsschluß am Veranstaltungstag. Es
gelten die Gemeinsamen Beförderungsbedingungen und Tarifbestimmungen.
(Benutzung der 1. Wagenklasse S-Bahn nur mit Zuschlag).

№ 93

Wichtiger Hinweis siehe Rückseite!

Kontroll-Abriß
№ 93

siehe Rückseite!

Kontroll-Abriß
№ 2786

Grateful Dead 1969

15 WAKE OF THE FLOOD 10/15/73

Bob Weir 10/16/1947

16 Last bar gigs, Club
Melk-Weg,
Amsterdam,
The Netherlands
10/15/81 – 10/16/81

East
Rutherford, NJ
10/16/89

17

18 St. Louis, MO
10/18/72

San Francisco,
CA 10/18/74

Minneapolis, MN.
Keith joins the band.
10/19/71

19 Barcelona, Spain.
"Europe '81" tour
ends. 10/19/81

San Francisco,
CA 10/19/68

20 Oklahoma City,
OK 10/19/73

The Dead stop
touring, pack in "Wall
of Sound." Mickey
returns. 10/20/74

Dizzy Gillespie 10/21/1917
Brent Mydland 10/21/1952

21 Berlin,
Germany
10/20/90

Chicago, IL
10/21/71

October

22

23

24

 San Francisco,
CA 10/25/69 **25**

 Indianapolis,
IN 10/25/73

 Miami, FL
10/26/89 **26**

27

 Cleveland, OH
10/28/72 **28**

October

29 Skullfuck 10/71

30  San Francisco, CA 10/30/68

St. Louis, MO 10/30/73

31

In the Dark 1987

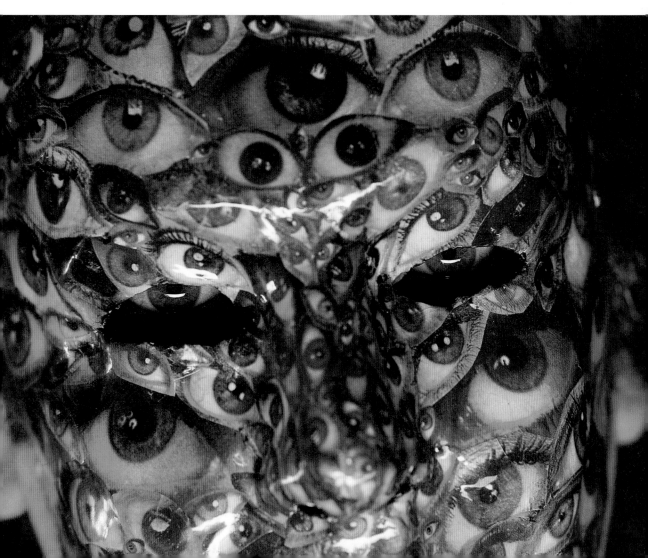

AMERICAN BEAUTY
11/70

1

 London,
England
11/1/90

2

3

4

 Port Chester,
NY 11/5/70

5

6

 San Francisco,
CA 11/7/69

7

 San Francisco,
CA 11/7/71

Bobby 1969

November

 San Francisco,
CA 11/8/69

 Port Chester,
NY 11/8/70

8

9

LIVE DEAD
11/10/69

10

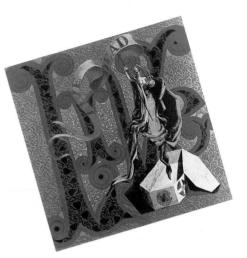

First appearance on
"Saturday Night Live."
Phil wears a large
"Hi Mom" button.
11/11/78

11

Neil Young 11/12/1945

12

13

"Shall we go,
you and I
while we can?
Through
the transitive nightfall
of diamonds?"

Dark Star
Robert Hunter

14

November

Garcia 1987

November

15 SHAKEDOWN STREET
11/15/78

EUROPE '72
11/72

 Austin, TX
11/15/71

16

17

18

19  Houston, TX
11/19/72

20

21

Billy 1979

22

Tom Constanten joins
The Dead in Athens,
OH 11/23/68

23

24

25 Bruce Hornsby 11/25/1955

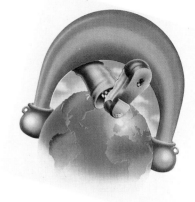

San Antonio,
TX 11/26/72

26

27

28

November

J. Garcia 1969

FALL
WINTER
TOUR

GRATEFUL DEAD 1988

ACCESS ALL AREAS

Laminate art by Tim Harris
Tie-die by Not Fade Away Graphics

Grateful Dead 1968

December

1

2

3

4   San Francisco,
CA 12/4/69

5   NYC, NY
12/5/71

6   Cleveland, OH
12/6/73

7

GRATEFUL DEAD

Billy and Pig 1966

December

8

9

10

San Francisco Mime Troupe benefit. First performance at Fillmore Auditorium, San Francisco, CA 12/10/65

Los Angeles, CA 12/10/69

11

Los Angeles, CA 12/11/69

San Francisco, CA 12/11/72

12

Denver, CO 12/12/90

13

Los Angeles, CA 12/13/67

14

Denver, CO 12/14/90

Oakland Coliseum,
Oakland, CA. First
show since Garcia's
recuperation.
12/15/86

15

 Long Beach,
CA 12/15/72

16

17

 Tampa, FL
12/18/73

18

19

 San Francisco,
CA 12/20/69

20

21

December

Grateful Dead 1968

22

23

24

25

26

27

28

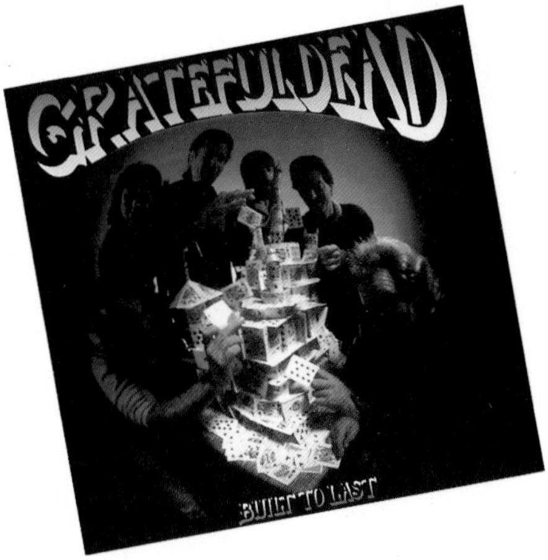

December

30 Boston, MA
12/30/69

31 Donna's first
performance with The
Dead. Winterland,
San Francisco, CA
12/31/71

The Grateful Dead
close Winterland, San
Francisco, CA
12/31/78

Built to Last
12/31/89

 San Francisco,
CA 12/31/68

San Francisco,
CA 12/31/78

Oakland, CA
12/31/81

Oakland, CA
12/31/89

 Oakland, CA
12/31/90

Chronology

Early 1965: Mother McCree's Uptown Jug Champions go electric and become the Warlocks. The band consists of Jerry Garcia, Bob Weir, Ron "Pig Pen" McKernan, Bill Kreutzmann and Dana Morgan, Jr.

May 5, 1965: The Warlocks play their first gig at Magoo's Pizza Parlor in Menlo Park, CA.

June 18, 1965: Phil Lesh replaces Dana Morgan, Jr. on bass at Frenchy's, Hayward, CA. The band gets fired the next night.

November 3, 1965: The Warlocks, as the "Emergency Crew," make their first studio recording at Golden State Studios in San Francisco; a demo for Autumn Records mogul, Tom Donahue. They don't get signed.

November, 1965: Due to Garcia's dictionary-induced flash of inspiration, the Warlocks change their name to the Grateful Dead.

December 4, 1965: San Jose Acid Test.

December 10, 1965: Mime Troupe Benefit. The Dead's first appearance at the Fillmore Auditorium.

December 11, 1965: Big Beat Acid Test, Palo Alto, CA.

December 18, 1965: Muir Beach Acid Test. Moved at the last minute from Stinson Beach. Owsley arrives and pushes chair back and forth around the floor.

January, 1966: Portland, OR Acid Test.

January 7, 1966: The Dead play the Matrix for the first time.

January 8, 1966: Fillmore Acid Test

January 14, 1966: Mime Troupe Benefit, Fillmore Auditorium. Billed on poster as "formerly the Warlocks."

January 22, 1966: Trips Festival, Longshoreman's Hall, San Francisco.

February 12, 1966: Watts Acid Test.

March 12, 1966: Pico Acid Test, Danish Center, Los Angeles, CA.

May 19, 1966: Straight Theater Benefit. The Dead's first appearance at the Avalon Ballroom.

May 28, 1966: "Hayfever" dance, Avalon Ballroom. The Dead's first Family Dog production.

July 16, 1966: Fillmore Auditorium: Joan Baez and Mimi Farina join the Dead onstage for "Midnight Hour."

July 29, 1966: P.N.E. Garden Auditorium, Vancouver, B.C., Canada. The Dead's first show outside the United States, outside California, for that matter.

July, 1966: The Dead's first single – "Don't Ease Me In/Stealin'" is released. Fails to make a dent on the charts.

Summer, 1966: Rancho Olompali: John Cipollina and Peter Albin make plans to throw Garcia in swimming pool. Nothing happens after John becomes otherwise occupied.

September 4, 1966: The Dead headline the Fillmore for the first time, over Quicksilver Messenger Service and Great Society.

September 16-17, 1966: Avalon Ballroom. Poster contains first use of "skeleton and roses" image.

September, 1966: The Grateful Dead move to 710 Ashbury Street, San Francisco.

October 2, 1966: The Dead play the San Francisco State Trips Festival. Fugitive Ken Kesey broadcasts to assembled multitudes.

October 6, 1966: LSD becomes illegal in California. The Dead play in Golden Gate Park Panhandle at the Love Pageant Rally (aka "Lunatic Protest Demonstration.")

October 31, 1966: The Dead, Quicksilver and Mimi Farina are scheduled to play the "Dance of Death" at California Hall, San Francisco. Along comes Ken Kesey with his own plans for an "Acid Test Graduation" at Winterland the same night, insisting that he can't do it without the Dead. Community distrust of Kesey puts an end to the

Winterland event and the Dead play California Hall after all.

December 20, 1966: The Dead open for Otis Redding at the Fillmore.

December 31, 1966: Fillmore Auditorium. The Dead's first New Year's Eve show, with the Jefferson Airplane and Quicksilver Messenger Service.

January 1, 1967: The Dead, tired from the night before, are rousted from bed by Digger Emmett Grogan and play at the Hell's Angels' "New Year's Day Wail" in the Panhandle.

January 13, 1967: The Dead are called upon to play second to the Mama's and the Papa's at Berkeley Community Theater, as Jose Feliciano couldn't make it in time for the first show. The Dead played BCT and came back to San Francisco for their previously scheduled gig at the Fillmore. Feliciano made it on time for the second show at BCT so the Dead didn't have to go back there.

January 14, 1967: Great Human Be-In, Polo Field, Golden Gate Park.

January, 1967: The Dead record their first album for Warner Bros. in Los Angeles.

March 3, 1967: "The First Annual Love Circus." The Dead play their first Winterland gig as picketers walk in front of the building protesting the outrageous ticket price ($3.50).

March 17, 1967: The Grateful Dead's first LP is released. An album release party is held at Fugazi Hall in San Francisco.

April 9, 1967: While a street party is going on, the Dead entertain the throngs from a third floor flat at the corner of Haight and Ashbury. The police shortly arrive and order everyone to move it to the Panhandle.

June 1, 1967: The Dead's first East Coast appearance at Tompkins Square Park in New York. The Dead stay through the 12th, playing at the Cafe A-Go-Go, the Cheetah and the Bandshell on the Mall in Central Park.

June 15, 1967: The Dead play at the "christening" of the Straight Theatre on Haight Street.

June 18, 1967: The Dead play at the Monterey Pop Festival after the Who and before Jimi Hendrix. While on stage, Phil Lesh and Peter Tork exchange a few words. The other two days of the festival, members of the Dead play on the free stage at Monterey Peninsula College along with such luminaries as Eric Burdon and Country Joe and the Fish.

June 21, 1967: Summer Solstice Celebration, Polo Field, Golden Gate Park.

June 28, 1967: The Grateful Dead's first appearance at Oakland Auditorium Arena, with Country Joe and the Fish, The Sons of Champlin, the Sparrow and – special guest stars – the Grass Roots.

July 23, 1967: Probably the night that Neal Cassady gave his famous rap at the Straight Theatre with backup by the Dead.

July 31, 1967: The first of six shows the Dead played at the O'Keefe Centre in Toronto with the Jefferson Airplane and Luke & the Apostles.

August 28, 1967: The Dead and Big Brother played Lindley Meadows in Golden Gate Park at the wake for popular Hell's Angel Chocolate George.

September 3-4, 1967: While woodshedding at Russian River writing new material the Dead play two gigs at the Rio Nido Dance Hall. Robert Hunter, newly returned from New Mexico, hears them play an instrumental "Dark Star" at one of these shows and immediately begins writing lyrics for it.

September 29, 1967: Straight Theatre, San Francisco. Bill Kreutzmann brings his friend Mickey Hart to the gig, who sits in on a second drum set for the second set: a two-hour "Alligator Caution." Mickey joins the band.

October 1, 1967: The Dead's first appearance at the Greek Theatre, U.C. Berkeley, a benefit for the Economic Opportunity Program with Charles Lloyd and Bola Sete.

October 2, 1967: The police raid 710 Ashbury. Bob Weir and Pig Pen, as well as some office staff and girlfriends, are arrested.

December 13, 1967: Shrine Auditorium, Los Angeles. The first known live performance of "Dark Star."

December 26, 1967: The Dead's first show at the Village Theater in New York, soon to become known as Fillmore East.

January 17, 1968: The Dead's first show at the Carousel Ballroom, San Francisco, a birthday party for Ben Franklin. The Dead and the Airplane subsequently take over the venue and operate it through June.

January 20, 1968: Eureka Municipal Auditorium, Eureka, CA. The Great Northwest Tour with Quicksilver begins, lasting through February 4.

March 3, 1968: The Dead play on a flatbed truck at the corner of Haight and Cole streets, as that part of Haight Street is closed to traffic.

March 18, 1968: Garcia jams with Traffic outside the KMPX studios on Green Street, San Francisco, after the station's staff had gone on strike.

May, 1968: "Dark Star/Born Cross-Eyed" is released.

May 3, 1968: The Dead play in the Low Library Plaza at Columbia University during student strike.

May 5, 1968: The Grateful Dead play in Central Park, New York with the Jefferson Airplane and the Butterfield Blues Band.

May 18, 1968: In between shows at the Shrine Auditorium in Los Angeles, the Dead and their crew fly up to San Jose to play at the Northern California Folk-Rock Festival.

June 14, 1968: The Dead's first appearance at Fillmore East under Bill Graham's auspices, with Kaleidoscope and Albert Collins.

September 2, 1968: Sky River Festival, Sultan, WA.

September 5, 1968: The Dead begin recording Aoxomoxoa.

September 20, 1968: The Dead are joined onstage at Berkeley Community Theater by Shankar Chosh and Vince Delgado for a rousing percussion jam.

October 8, 1968: The first of several performances at the Matrix by a band that's come to be known as "Mickey Hart and the Hartbeats," essentially the Grateful Dead without Pig Pen and Bob Weir, and with special guests.

October 21, 1968: In the midst of a debauched party at the Jefferson Airplane house, Garcia and Hart jam with Jorma Kaukonen, Jack Casady and Spencer Dryden.

November 23, 1968: Tom Constanten joins the Dead in Athens, Ohio after being discharged from the Air Force the day before.

December 6, 1968: The "Quaker City Rock Festival": The Dead's first performance at the Spectrum in Philadelphia.

December 31, 1968: The Dead's first New Year's show at Winterland, with Quicksilver Messenger Service, It's a Beautiful Day, and Santana.

February 27, 1969: Fillmore West, San Francisco. The night the Dead performed the "Dark Star" and "St. Stephen" that later appeared on "Live Dead."

March 15, 1969: The Dead play the "Black and White Ball" at the Hilton Hotel in San Francisco.

April 6, 1969: The Dead's last show at the Avalon Ballroom, broadcast live on KPFA-FM.

May 7, 1969: The Grateful Dead and the Jefferson Airplane play at the Polo Field in Golden Gate Park.

May 11, 1969: Santana sits in with the Dead at the Aztec Bowl, San Diego State University.

June 7, 1969: Janis Joplin joins the band during "Turn On Your Lovelight" at the Fillmore West.

June 11, 1969: The first performance of "Bobby Ace and the Cards from the Bottom of the Deck" at California Hall.

June 13, 1969: Ronnie Hawkins sits in on "Lovelight" at the Fresno Convention Center.

June 20, 1969: "Aoxomoxoa" is released.

June 22, 1969: The Dead appear on "Playboy after Dark" and make Hugh Hefner look like an idiot.

August 16, 1969: The Dead play Woodstock in the midst of much electronic turmoil.

November 10, 1969: "Live Dead" is released.

November 15, 1969: The Dead play a Vietnam War Moratorium benefit at the Lanai Theater, Crockett, CA.

December 6, 1969: The Altamont disaster, which the Dead didn't even get to play at and maybe save things somewhat. They didn't play the Fillmore West that night, either.

December 10, 1969: Stephen Stills sits in with the band at the Thelma Theater, Los Angeles.

December 21, 1969: The Dead's last performance at the Fillmore Auditorium.

January 30, 1970: Tom Constanten's last performance as a member of the Grateful Dead, at a New Orleans venue called the Warehouse. After the gig the band got busted at their hotel.

February, 1970: The Dead record "Workingman's Dead."

February 11, 1970: Duane and Gregg Allman, along with Fleetwood Mac's Peter Green, sit in with the Dead during the first show of an incredible run.

March 17, 1970: The Dead jam with the Buffalo Philharmonic Orchestra at the Kleinhans Music Hall in Buffalo, N.Y.

April 9, 1970: The Dead begin a four night series at the Fillmore West during which they have to follow Miles Davis.

May 6, 1970: The Dead play Kresge Plaza, M.I.T. during the nationwide campus strikes protesting the Kent State killings.

May 24, 1970: The Dead's first European Performance: The Hollywood Festival, Newcastle-Under-Lyme, England.

May, 1970: "Workingman's Dead" is released.

June 13, 1970: Honolulu Civic Auditorium. Gary Duncan and Dino Valenti sit in.

June 27, 1970: The beginning of the Great Canadian Train Ride.

July 16, 1970: Euphoria Ballroom, San Rafael, CA. Janis joins in "Lovelight."

August 30, 1970: "Calibration," KQED Studios, San Francisco. The world's first TV broadcast with an FM simulcast. The Dead played five songs.

September, 1970: The Dead begin recording "American Beauty."

October 4, 1970: The Dead, along with the Jefferson Airplane, Quicksilver Messenger Service, Hot Tuna and New Riders of the Purple Sage, played the first ever TV broadcast of a live concert with a quadraphonic FM simulcast, originating at Winterland. As luck would have it, Janis Joplin died that night. Not only that, before this set of shows was over, Marty Balin left the Airplane and John Cipollina left Quicksilver.

November 16, 1970: Jorma Kaukonen sits in at Fillmore East.

November 20, 1970: Jorma Kaukonen sits in at Rochester.

November 23, 1970: Anderson Theater, New York Hell's Angels benefit. The Dead were joined by Stevie Winwood, Chris Wood and Jim Capaldi from Traffic, Ramblin' Jack Elliott, Will Scarlett and supposedly others.

November, 1970: "American Beauty" is released.

February 18, 1971: Capitol Theater, Port Chester, N.Y. Mickey Hart's last gig with the band for quite a while. A bunch of new songs were premiered this night; a successful experiment in dream telepathy was also conducted. Even so, the attempted live recording didn't pan out, at least from the band's point of view.

March 5, 1971: The Black Panther benefit at Oakland Auditorium, one of the more unusual fundraisers the Dead were talked into doing.

April 26, 1971: Fillmore East. Special guest – Duane Allman.

April 27, 1971: Fillmore East. Special Guests – The Beach Boys.

April 28, 1971: Fillmore East. Special guest – Tom Constanten.

April 29, 1971: The Dead's last appearance at Fillmore East. No special guests.

May 29, 1971: A large barrel of spiked Kool-Aid almost results in the closure of Winterland.

June 21, 1971: The Dead go to France to play at a festival, which gets rained out, so they play at the grounds of Chateau D'Herouville instead, opening for Light Sound Dimension.

July 4, 1971: The Dead's last appearance at Fillmore West, part of a week-long extravaganza. Every night it is broadcast on the radio; within a month bootleg LPs start appearing in Bay Area record stores.

August 26, 1971: Gaelic Park, Bronx, N.Y. The last appearance of the original five-man Grateful Dead. Pig Pen bows out for awhile due to his failing health.

October 6, 1971: "Skullfuck" is released.

October 19, 1971: Northrop Auditorium, University of Minnesota, Minneapolis. Keith Godchaux debuts with the band on piano.

December 1, 1971: Boston Music Hall. Pig Pen is back in the lineup.

December 31, 1971: Winterland. Donna Godchaux's first appearance with the Dead, helping out on "One More Saturday Night."

March 5, 1972: Indian benefit at Winterland. Pig Pen's last gig in the Bay Area.

April 7, 1972: The Europe '72 tour starts at Wembly Empire Pool.

May 5, 1972: The Dead were supposed to play the Lille Opera House but the equipment truck was still in Paris, having been sabotaged by angry French students. The band had to make a quick getaway but returned on May 13 to play a magical show at the Lille Fairgrounds.

May 26, 1972: The Strand Lyceum, London. The end of the Europe Tour and last time Pig Pen sang with the Grateful Dead.

May, 1972: "Ace" is released.

June 17, 1972: Hollywood Bowl. Pig Pen's last appearance with the Grateful Dead, playing but not singing.

August 27, 1972: The Dead play three sets for the Springfield Creamery at the Old Rennaisance Fair Grounds in Veneta, OR. It gets so hot that most of the audience take their clothes off.

October 9, 1972: Winterland. A benefit for the Grateful Dead roadies (they needed money to buy a house) featuring the Dead and the New Riders. Grace Slick comes out and sings a little; following the music is a basketball game between the Dead roadies and BGP called the "Toilet Bowl."

November, 1972: "Europe '72" is released.

February 9, 1973: Maples Pavilion, Stanford University. The Dead unveil a new sound system as well as lots of new songs. Unfortunately, most of the system gets smoked two seconds into the show.

March 8, 1973: Ron "Pig Pen" McKernan dies at his home in Corte Madera, CA.

March 23, 1973: Cow Palace, Daly City, CA. The Dead debut the final version of the "Wall of Sound."

March 25, 1973: The Dead begin recording "Mars Hotel."

May 26, 1973: The Dead play three sets in the sun at Kezar Stadium in Golden Gate Park, following the New Riders and Waylon Jennings. Faces are peeling for a week.

June 10, 1973: In scorching heat at RFK Stadium in Washington, D.C., the Dead are joined onstage by the Allman Bros. and Merl Saunders.

June 23, 1973: Jai-Alai Fronton, Miami, FL. During the set break Phil and computer whiz Ned Lagin perform abstract electronic music. This takes place at most shows for the rest of the year.

June 27, 1973: "Grateful Dead from the Mars Hotel" is released.

July 13, 1973: "Bear's Choice" is released.

July 27, 1973: The Dead played a two hour soundcheck in front of those already assembled at the Grand Prix Racecourse in Watkins Glen, N.Y. that was, by many accounts, better than the actual show they played the next day in front of 750,000 people.

August, 1973: The Dead begin recording "Wake of the Flood."

September 9, 1973: Europe Tour starts in London, ends in Paris on the 21st.

September 11, 1973: William & Mary College, Williamsburg, VA. Starting this night and lasting until the end of the tour in Buffalo on the 26th, Martin Fierro and Joe Ellis play horns on some songs.

October 15, 1973: "Wake of the Flood" is released.

October 20, 1973: Winterland. The Dead's last show before a two year break from touring. Mickey Hart rejoins the band at the second set.

December 19, 1973: Curtis Hixon Convention Hall, Tampa, FL. Most of show released in 1994 as "Dicks Picks Vol.1."

January 1975: The Dead begin recording "Blues for Allah."

March 23, 1975: The Dead, along with many others, play the SNACK (Students Need Athletics, Culture and Kicks) benefit at Kezar Stadium.

June 17, 1975: The Dead play a benefit for the family of poster artist Bob Fried at Winterland.

August 13, 1975: The Dead play an invitation only party at the Great American Music Hall, San Francisco, in conjunction with a Billboard magazine convention. This gig was released in 1991 as "One from the Vault."

September 28, 1975: The Dead and the Jefferson Starship play on an overcast day in Lindley Meadows, Golden Gate Park.

January, 1976: "Reflections" is released.

May, 1976: The Dead begin rehearsals for a return to live performances.

June 3, 1976: Paramount Theater, Portland, OR. The Dead return to live performance.

June 26, 1976: "Steal Your Face" is released.

July 18, 1976: Orpheum Theatre, San Francisco. Bill Graham and a bevy of bathing beauties toast the band at the start of the second set.

October 9-10, 1976: The Dead open for the Who both days at Oakland Stadium. Scalpers, who bought up tickets thinking they would make a killing, wind up trading tickets for as little as a pack of cigarettes.

January, 1977: The Dead begin recording "Terrapin Station."

June 1, 1977: The "Grateful Dead Movie" premiers in New York.

July 27, 1977: "Terrapin Station" is released.

September 3, 1977: The Dead, Marshall Tucker and the New Riders play for 150,000 at Raceway Park, Englishtown, NJ.

January 6, 1978: Swing Auditorium, San Bernardino, CA. Jerry loses his voice during the first set. For the second set and for the next two shows in San Diego, Bob sings most of the songs.

April 6, 1978: The drums becomes a standard fixture at almost all shows from this point on.

June 25, 1978: Autzen Stadium, Eugene, OR. Ken Babbs delivers a rap during drums.

July 7, 1978: The Grateful Dead's first show at Red Rocks Amphitheatre, Morrison, CO.

August, 1978: The Dead begin recording "Shakedown Street."

September 14-16, 1978: The Dead perform at the Gizah Sound and Light Theater, Cairo, Egypt, in the shadow of the Sphinx and the Pyramids. Hamza El-Din opens the first sets of the first two nights and the second set of the third, which is graced by a lunar eclipse.

October 17-20, 1978: The Dead play Winterland with great enthusiasm, slides of the Egypt trip being projected above them. Hamza opens the first sets of the last two nights.

November 11, 1978: The Dead's first appearance on "Saturday Night Live."

November 15, 1978: "Shakedown Street" is released.

November 17, 1978: The Dead play their first acoustic set in eight years at Loyola University in Chicago.

November 24, 1978: Capitol Theatre, Passaic, N.J. During a hot show being broadcast nationally, Garcia starts losing his voice. The rest of the tour is canceled.

December 30, 1978: Pauley Pavilion, U.C.L.A. Hamza El-Din and Lee Oskar sit in.

December 31, 1978: Headlining over the New Riders and the Blues Brothers, the Dead close Winterland, playing from midnight to 6 am.

January 7, 1979: The Dead's first show at Madison Square Garden, rescheduled from November.

February 17, 1979: Oakland Coliseum Arena. The "Rock for Life" benefit, Keith and Donna's last gig with the Dead.

April 22, 1979: Spartan Stadium, San Jose, CA. Brent Mydland takes over on keyboards.

July, 1979: The Dead begin recording "Go to Heaven."

August 5, 1979: During the second of two shows at Oakland Auditorium, Hamza El-Din sits in.

December 31, 1979: Oakland Auditorium. John Cipollina joins the Dead for the last half of the third set.

January 13, 1980: Oakland Coliseum Arena. The Dead headline over Jefferson Starship, Joan Baez, the Beach Boys and Santana at a Cambodian Refugee benefit. The Dead are joined onstage by Carlos Santana, John Cipollina and Greg Errico.

March 30, 1980: John Belushi sings on "U.S. Blue" at the Capitol Theatre, Passaic, N.J.

April 1, 1980: Capitol Theatre, Passaic, N.J. The Dead open with Bobby on keyboards, Brent and Jerry on drums, Billy on bass, Mickey on rhythm guitar and vocals and Phil on lead guitar. Only Bobby seemed to know what he was doing.

April 5, 1980: The Dead's second appearance on "Saturday Night Live."

April 28, 1980: "Go to Heaven" is released.

June 12, 1980: Memorial Coliseum, Portland OR. The Dead play "Fire on the Mountain" as, unbeknownst to everyone at the show, Mt. St. Helens erupts.

June 19-21, 1980: The Dead play West High Auditorium in Anchorage, Alaska during almost 24-hour sunlight.

July 23, 1980: Keith Godchaux dies of injuries sustained in a car crash.

September 25, 1980: The Dead begin a run of shows starting with an acoustic set followed by two electric sets. Starting off with fifteen shows at the Warfield Theater in San Francisco, the band moves on to play two shows in New Orleans and eight more at Radio City Music Hall in New York, culminating in a Halloween night radio broadcast. The Dead wind up getting two albums and two videos out of this.

December 6, 1980: The Dead play an acoustic set for handicapped children at the Mill Valley Recreation Center.

December 13-14, 1980: Long Beach Arena. Flora Purim and Airto Moreira join in both nights, plus Matt Kelly on the second.

December 31, 1980: Oakland Auditorium. Another New Year's show with John Cipollina and Matt Kelly.

March 20, 1981: The Dead begin a short European jaunt at the Rainbow Theater in London.

March 28, 1981: Grugahalle, Essen, West Germany. The Dead and the Who play a show that is broadcast both on TV and the radio. The Dead are joined onstage by Pete Townshend and the Flying Karamazov Bros.

April 1, 1981: "Reckoning" is released.

May 7, 1981: The Dead play acoustic on the "Tomorrow Show."

August, 1981: "Dead Set" is released.

September 11, 1981: The yearly Greek Theatre weekend tradition begins.

September 30, 1981: The Europe '81 tour begins in Edinburgh, Scotland, ending in Barcelona on October 19.

October 15-16, 1981: With time on their hands due to two cancelled French shows, the Dead play for 400 people on borrowed instruments at the Melk Weg in Amsterdam. Bob and Jerry had checked the place out on the 11th.

December 12, 1981: "Dance for Disarmament," Fiesta Hall, County Fairgrounds, San Mateo, CA. The Dead back Joan Baez acoustically followed by their own electric set. The acoustic set contained new material that the Dead and Baez recorded, but never released in that form. Joan joined the boys again on December 30th and 31st.

December 31, 1981: Oakland Auditorium. Possibly the longest Grateful Dead concert ever, beginning with an acoustic set backing Joan Baez followed by three electric sets.

April 13, 1982: Jerry and Bob appear on the "David Letterman Show."

May 28, 1982: At a Vietnam veterans' benefit, the Dead play at the first concert ever in San Francisco's Moscone Center. The venue turns out to be an acoustic nightmare. Playing between Country Joe McDonald and Jefferson Starship, the Dead are joined onstage by Flora & Airto, John Cipollina and Boz Scaggs.

August 8, 1982: The Dead play in Veneta, OR again for the "Second Decadenal Field Trip." Once again, it's too hot to keep one's clothes on.

September 5, 1982: Glen Helen Regional Park, Devore, CA. The Dead play much earlier in the day than they're used to at the "Us Festival."

October 9, 1982: The Dead's first appearance at the incredible Frost Amphitheatre, Stanford University.

November 26, 1982: The Dead play even earlier in the morning than they're used to at the Jamaica World Music Festival.

December 30-31, 1982: Oakland Auditorium. Sitting in both days are Etta James and the Tower of Power horns on some old Pig Pen numbers. These are the Dead's last gigs at Oakland Auditorium before its renovation and name change.

March 2, 1983: San Francisco Civic Auditorium. Jerry and Bob play acoustic at the Bay Area Music Awards ("Bammies"). Perhaps it was here that they realized this would be a good substitute venue for Oakland Auditorium.

April 16-17, 1983: Meadowlands Arena, East Rutherford, NJ. Stephen Stills sits in both nights with the "greatest garage band in the world."

May 15, 1983: Greek Theatre. The Dead are joined by Flora and Airto, Billy Cobham and John Cipollina.

October 31, 1983: Marin County Veterans' Auditorium, San Rafael, CA. Airto plays the entire length of this incredible show. Alwo, Wavy Gravy is seen in his Halloween costume – a suit and tie.

December 31, 1983: San Francisco Civic Auditorium. The Dead are joined for the third set by Rick Danko, Maria Muldaur and John Cipollina.

May 8, 1984: Hult Center, Eugene, OR. Kesey and Babbs bring out the Thunder Machine during drums.

June 9, 1984: The Dead's first show at Cal Expo Amphitheatre, Sacramento, CA. Temperatures are ridiculous.

June 21, 1984: The Dead play a SEVA benefit at the Kingswood Music Theatre in Maple, Ontario, Canada. Joined for the third set by The Band, this show was broadcast everywhere.

July 13, 1984: Greek Theatre. The Dead play "Dark Star" as an encore while moonscapes are projected on a screen above them. Right before this happens a shooting star is sighted.

July 15, 1984: Greek Theatre. John Cipollina is unable to sit in with the Dead since he has to play with the Dinosaurs in Golden Gate Park.

October 27, 1984: Berkeley Community Theater. The Tapers' Section is instituted.

June 14, 1985: Greek Theatre. The Dead's "official" 20th anniversary show. Before the boys come out the first part of "Sgt. Pepper" is played extremely loud. This causes a large part of the P.A. to die during the first set.

December 31, 1985: Oakland Coliseum Arena. Baba Olatunji plays with the Dead during a nationwide TV and FM broadcast.

February 11-12, 1986: Henry J. Kaiser Convention Center, Oakland, CA. The Neville Brothers sit in with the Dead at what used to be Oakland Auditorium.

April 21, 1986: Berkeley Community Theatre. That night Brent did not allow drums to take place.

July 2, 7, 1986: While the Dead are touring with Dylan and Tom Petty, Dylan sits in at Akron and RFK.

July 10, 1986: Garcia falls into diabetic coma, complicated by a systemic infection caused by an abscessed tooth. An extremely serious, life-threatening situation. Jerry manages an amazing recovery within days.

December 15, 1986: Oakland Coliseum Arena. The Dead's first show since Jerry's illness. There's not a dry eye in the house. The Neville Bros. sit in the next night, again at the Kaiser on the 30th.

"We can share what we got of yours cause
we done shared all of mine."

Jack Straw, Robert Hunter

March 3, 1987: The Dead are joined during Mardi Gras at the Kaiser by the members of the Dirty Dozen Brass Band.

July 4-26, 1987: The Dead play six shows with a set backing Bob Dylan.

August 13, 1987: The Dead's last show at Red Rocks.

August 22-23, 1987: Santana sits in with the Dead both days at Calaveras.

October 2, 1987: The Dead's first appearance at Shoreline Amphitheatre, Mountain View, CA on the 20th anniversary of the bust at 710 Ashbury. They do "Truckin'."

December 31, 1987: Oakland Coliseum Arena: Sitting in with the Dead are Ramblin' Jack Elliott, David Nelson and members of the Neville Brothers.

March 17, 1988: Hamza El-Din joins in at the Kaiser.

June 25, 1988: Buckeye Lake Music Center, Hebron, OH. Bruce Hornsby sits in with the Dead for the first time.

July 16, 1988: Jerry sits in with Zero at the bandshell in Golden Gate Park, zooming to the Greek Theatre afterwards to play with the Dead. He plays "Knockin' on Heaven's Door" twice, in different keys.

July 31, 1988: Laguna Seca Recreation Area, Monterey, CA. David Hidalgo of Los Lobos sits in.

October 18, 1988: The Neville Brothers and the Bangles sit in with the Dead in New Orleans.

December 24, 1988: The Dead play a Rainforest benefit at Madison Square Garden with a cast of thousands.

January 31, 1989: "Dylan and the Dead" is released.

February 7, 1989: The Dead's last show at the Kaiser.

February 12, 1989: Also at the Forum, the Dead are joined by Spencer Davis and Bob Dylan.

March 22, 1989: Jerry and Bob play at a benefit for Artist Rights Today at the Gift Center in San Francisco. Jerry also sits in with Country Joe McDonald.

May 7, 1989: The Dead's last show at the Frost Amphitheatre.

May 27, 1989: Oakland Coliseum Stadium. The Dead play an AIDS benefit. Earlier, Jerry and Bob help back John Fogerty.

July 10, 1989: The Neville Brothers sit in with the Dead at Giants Stadium.

August 19, 1989: The Dead's last show at the Greek Theatre.

October 8-9, 1989: The Dead play two gigs at Hampton Coliseum as "formerly the Warlocks." Much yummy material is revived.

October 31, 1989: "Built to Last" is released.

December 6, 1989: The Dead play an Earthquake Relief Fund benefit at Oakland Coliseum Arena.

December 10, 1989: Spencer Davis and Bruce Hornsby sit in at the Great Western Forum, Inglewood, CA.

December 27, 1989: The Dead are joined onstage by Clarence Clemons at Oakland Coliseum Arena.

December 28, 1989: The Dead are joined at Oakland by Willie Green of the Neville Brothers.

December 30, 1989: The Dead are joined at Oakland by Airto.

December 31, 1989: The Dead are joined at Oakland by Airto, Bonnie Raitt and Taro Hart.

February 27, 1990: The Dead are joined for Mardi Gras by Michael Doucet And Beausoliel at Oakland.

March 29, 1990: Nassau Coliseum, Uniondale, NY. The Dead are joined by Branford Marsalis for an amazing performance.

July 23, 1990: World Music Theatre, Tinley Park, ILL. Brent Mydland's last performance.

July 26, 1990: Brent Mydland dies at the age of 37.

September 7, 1990: Vince Welnick joins the Grateful Dead on keyboards at Richfield Coliseum, Richfield, OH.

September 15, 1990: Madison Square Garden. Bruce Hornsby's first gig as a member of the Grateful Dead.

September, 1990: "Without a Net" is released.

October 13, 1990: The Europe '90 Tour Begins in Stockholm, ending November 1, in London.

December 3, 1990: Sikiru Adepoju sits in the the Dead in Oakland.

December 4, 1990: Huey Lewis sits in with the Dead in Oakland.

December 27, 1990: Hamza El-Din sits in with the Dead in Oakland.

December 31, 1990: Hamza El-Din and Branford Marsalis sit in with the Dead in Oakland.

February 20, 1991: Baba Olatunji and Sikiru Adepoju sit in with the Dead in Oakland.

February 21, 1991: Airto sits in with the Dead in Oakland.

April 15, 1991: "One From the Vault" is released

April 28, 1991: Carlos Santana sits in with the Dead in Las Vegas.

September 10, 1991: Branford Marsalis joins in at Madison Square Garden.

October 25, 1991: Bill Graham dies in a helicopter crash.

October 27, 1991: The Dead play Oakland Coliseum Arena. David Graham talks about his father at the break. Carlos Santana and Gary Duncan jam with the Dead during the second set.

October 31, 1991: Gary Duncan once again jams with the Dead during the second set at Oakland. Ken Kesey comes out and delivers a rap during "Dark Star."

November 3, 1991: The Dead, as well as Crosby Stills, Nash & Young, Santana, Journey and others, play at the Polo Field in Golden Gate Park at a memorial concert for Bill Graham. The Dead are themselves joined by John Popper and Neil Young, also serving as backup band for John Fogerty on some Creedence songs.

December 30-31, 1991: Airto sits in with the Dead at Oakland. The 31st is also the Dead's last New Year's show, at least for now.

March 24, 1992: Bruce Hornsby's last show as a member of the Grateful Dead.

May 12, 1992: "Two From the Vault" is released.

May 31, 1992: Steve Miller jams with the Dead in Las Vegas, and at most shows on Summer Tour.

June 25, 1992: James Cotton joins in with the band in Chicago.

July 1, 1992: Norton Buffalo sits in at Buckeye Lake.

August, 1992: Garcia gets sick, forcing cancellation of all shows through October. Jerry gets better and is healthier than ever.

January 26, 1993: Carlos Santana jams with the Dead at Chinese New Year show in Oakland.

February 23, 1993: Ornette Coleman and Graham Wiggins sit in on second set in Oakland for Mardi Gras.

March 11, 1993: Ken Nordine raps during drumz in Rosemont, IL.

April 1, 1993: At Nassau Coliseum, Barney the Purple Dinosaur plays bass on "Iko Iko."

September 20, 1993: Edie Brickell wails with the Dead at Madison Square Garden.

September 22, 1993: David Murray and James Cotton join the Dead for an amazing show at the Garden.

September 9, 1993: Ornette Coleman and Airto & Flora sit in with the Dead at the Los Angeles Sports Arena.

December 10, 1993: Branford Marsalis plays with the Dead for the entire show at L.A. Sports Arena.

—Chronology compiled by Mike Dolgushkin and Dead Base.

J. Garcia 1990

"Hand me my old guitar
Pass the whiskey 'round
Want you to tell everybody you meet
the Candyman's in town."

Candyman
Robert Hunter

Because a project like this takes the help and cooperation of many people, I would like to mention as many of them as possible.

My first thanks go to the people who helped me get started with this project: Robert Hunter for writing truly great lyrics that make listening to the Dead compelling; my good friend and cosmic consultant, Nancy "Willie" Wilson for showing me a "really" good time at many shows over the years; Anne Carey for her ticket stubs and for giving me a new and appreciative perspective on the wonderful world of "Dead Heads"; because he is always there, David Gans; and David Barich, Karen Pike, Lisa Howard, and Nion McEvoy at Chronicle Books. And the winners for excellence in design are Tom Ingalls, Kendra Lawrence and Carole Selig. A big Grateful Dead thank you to Charlie Winton for the terrific input. See you backstage Charlie!

The materials and information in this book were collected from many dedicated supporters. The guys at Dead Base, John W. Scott, Stu Nixon, and especially Mike Dolgushkin, provided a wealth of data. Steve Marcus and Frankie Accardi of the Grateful Dead ticket office gave me access to their personal collections. Tim Harris provided access to his rare collection of fantastic laminate designs. Martin Leffer, of Not Fade Away Graphics, provided some of the tie-dyes. The fine photographic printing was done by David and Cissy Spindler (black and white) of Spindler photographics and David Peterson (color) of Faulkner Color Lab.

Thanks also for the cooperation and contributions of Calico, Bill Belmont, Patricia Harris, Blair Jackson, Jon McIntire, Dennis McNally, Danny Rifkin, Cameron Sears, Tony Secunda, Jan Simmons, Sue Swanson, Robbie Taylor, and Brian Kemble.

The entire Grateful Dead organization has been terrifically supportive, but most of all I'd like to thank the ladies in the office for their continual help. Eileen Law has been particularly helpful, along with Annette Flowers, Diane Geoppo, Janet Knudsen, Cassidy Law, Nancy Mallonee, Mary Jo Meinolf, Maruska Nelson, Basia Raizene, Jeanni Rasmussen, and Sue Stephens.

Of course, no thank you list would be complete without mentioning the intrepid crew: Bill Candelario, John Cutler, Billy Grillo, Bill Langevin, Steve Parish, Harry Popick, Bob Bralove, and most of all "Ram Rod" Shurtliff for his steadfast friendship.

And to my friend and colleague Stacy Quinn, mere words cannot express my gratitude for what you have done — believing in this book and giving "sunshine" a new day!!!

Gratefully yours.

Herb Greene

Notes, Sets, Names & Addresses

If you can read this incredibly small type, we hope your trip is as good as your eyesight!